A PEACEFUL JOURNEY

van Meeboer

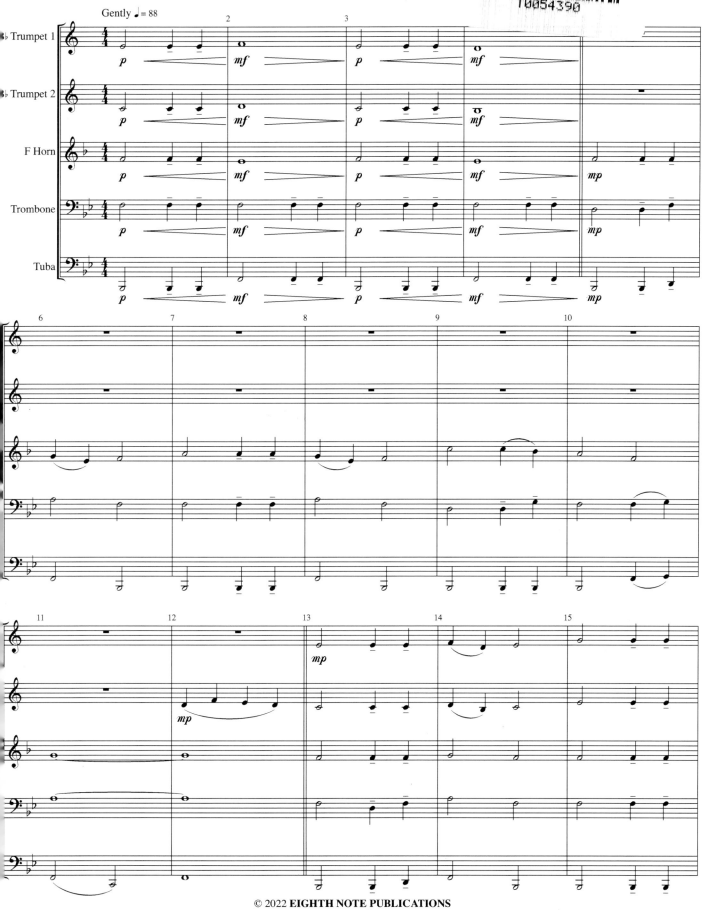

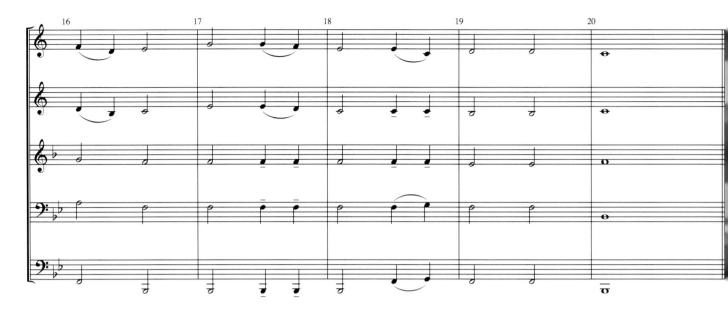

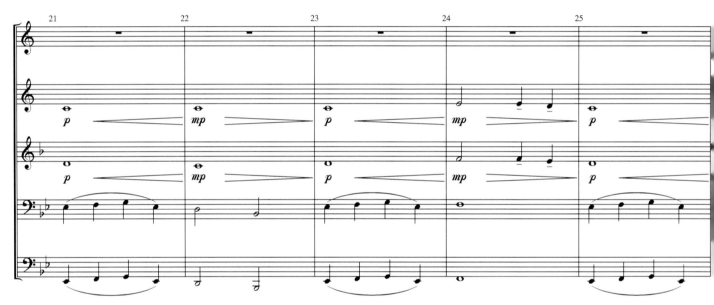

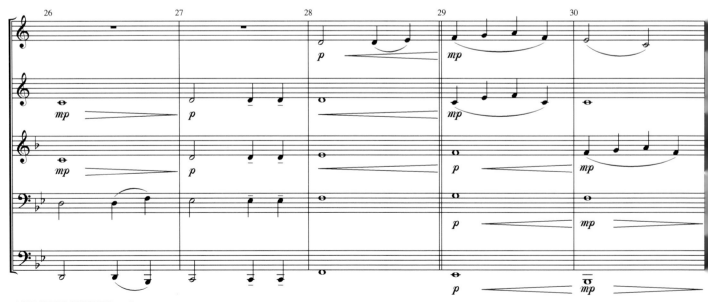

B♭ Trumpet 1

A PEACEFUL JOURNEY

Ryan Meeboer

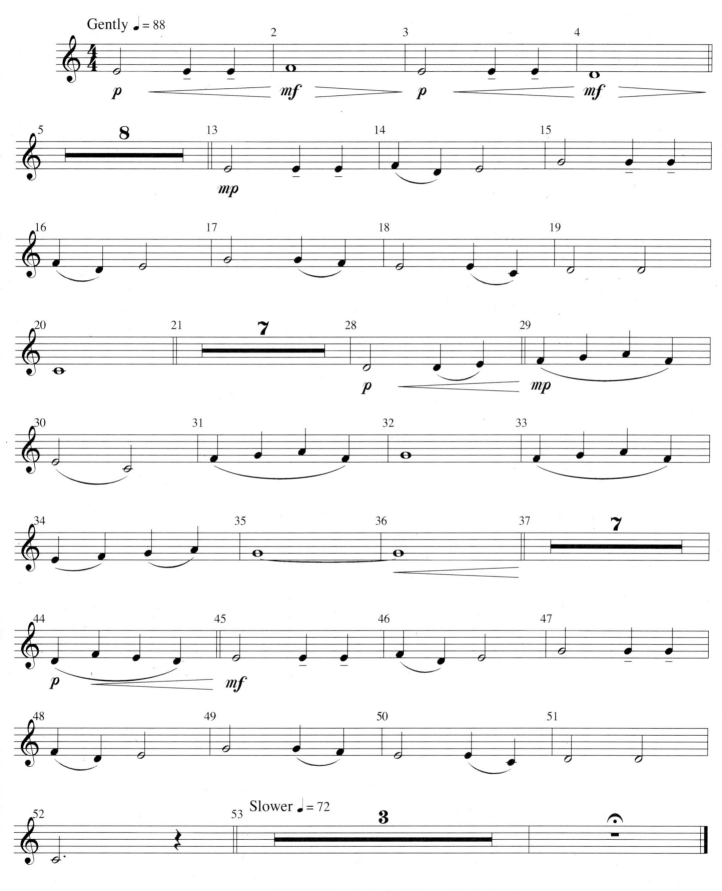

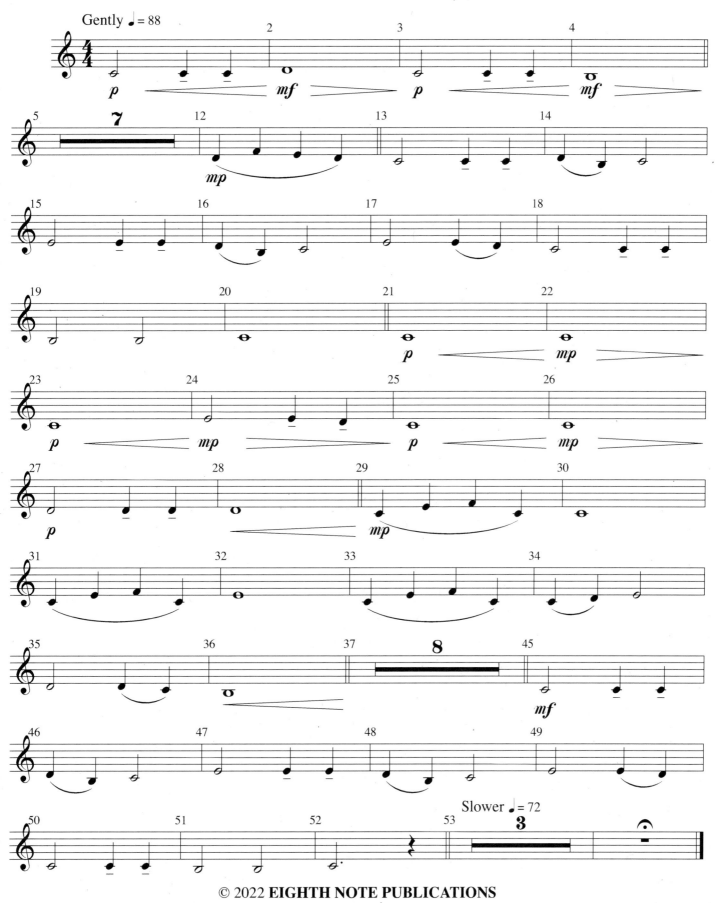

B♭ Trumpet 2

A PEACEFUL JOURNEY

Ryan Meeboer

F Horn

A PEACEFUL JOURNEY

Ryan Meeboer

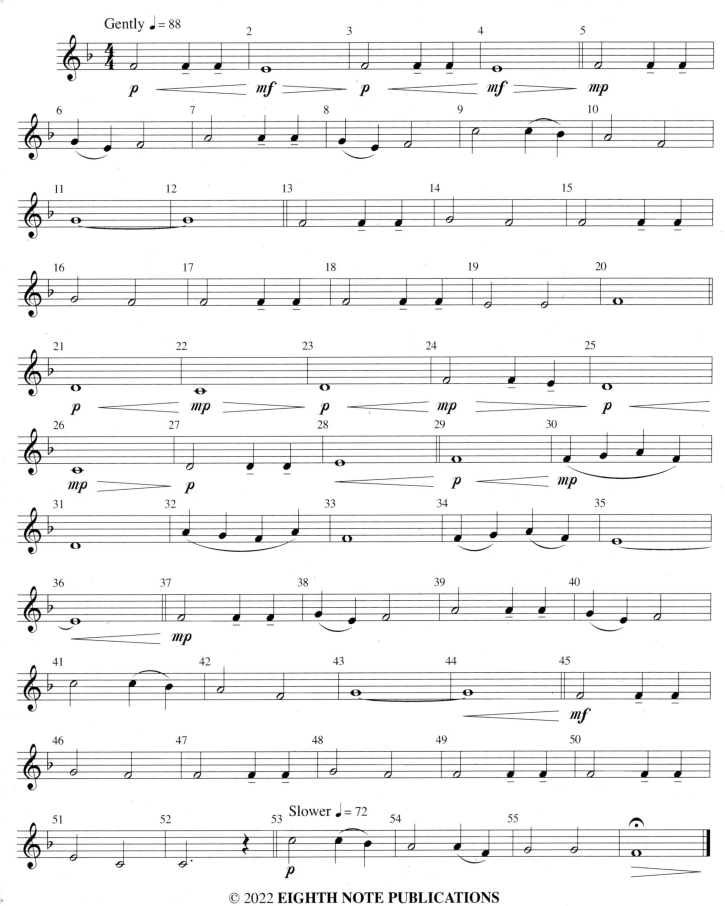

Trombone

A PEACEFUL JOURNEY

Ryan Meeboer

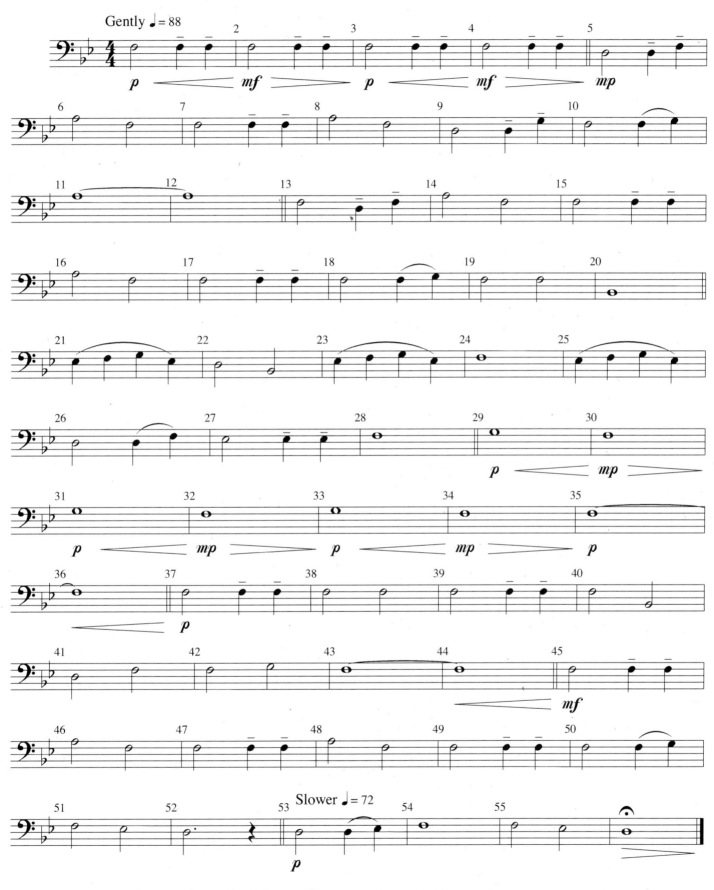

Tuba

A PEACEFUL JOURNEY

Ryan Meeboer

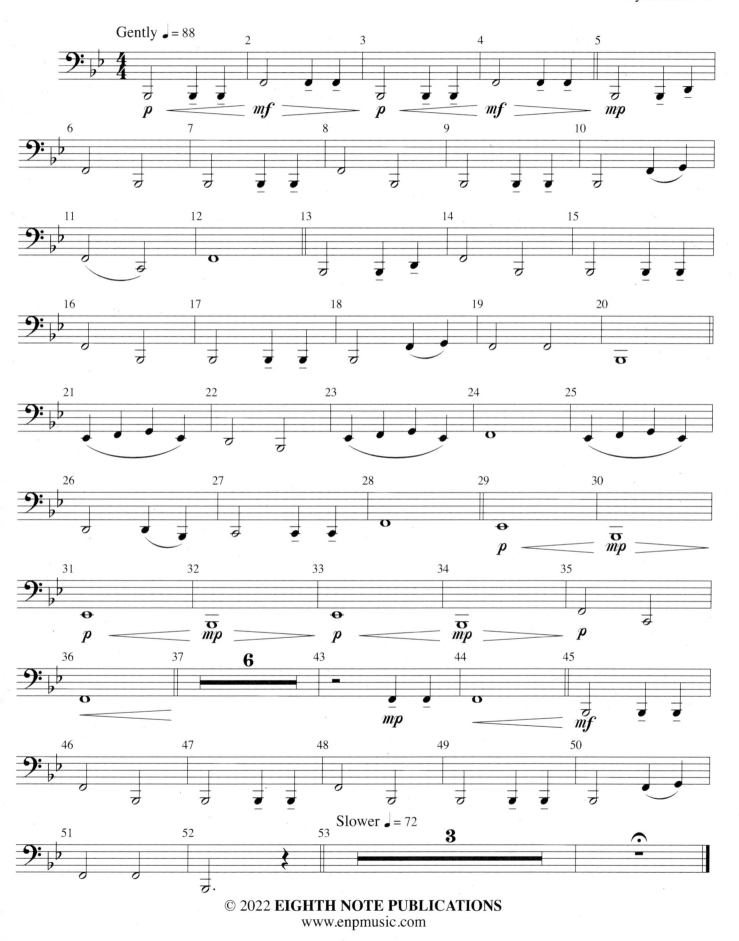

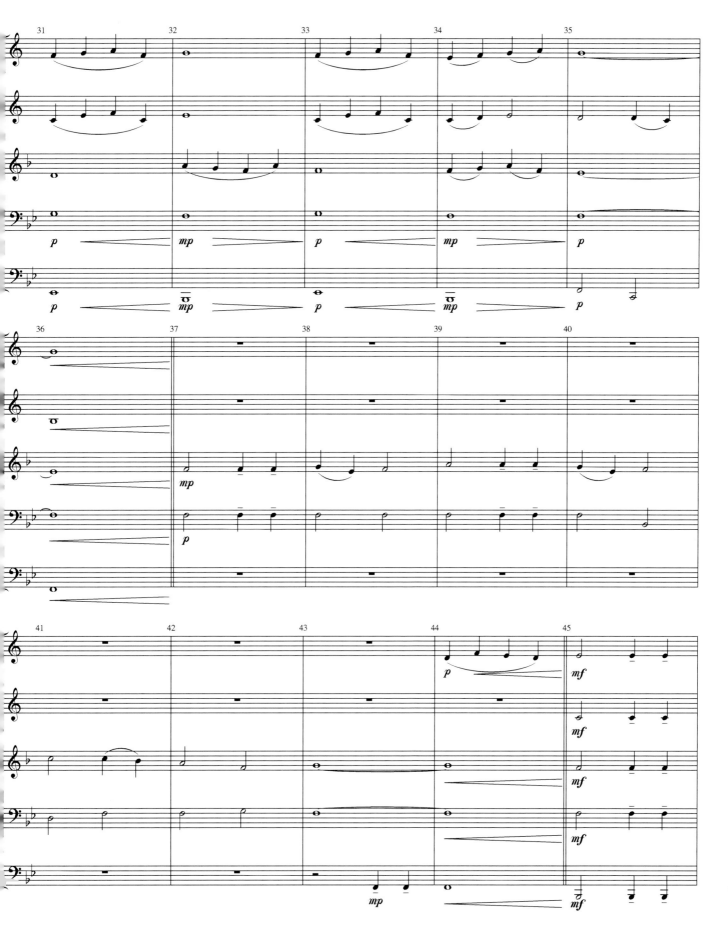

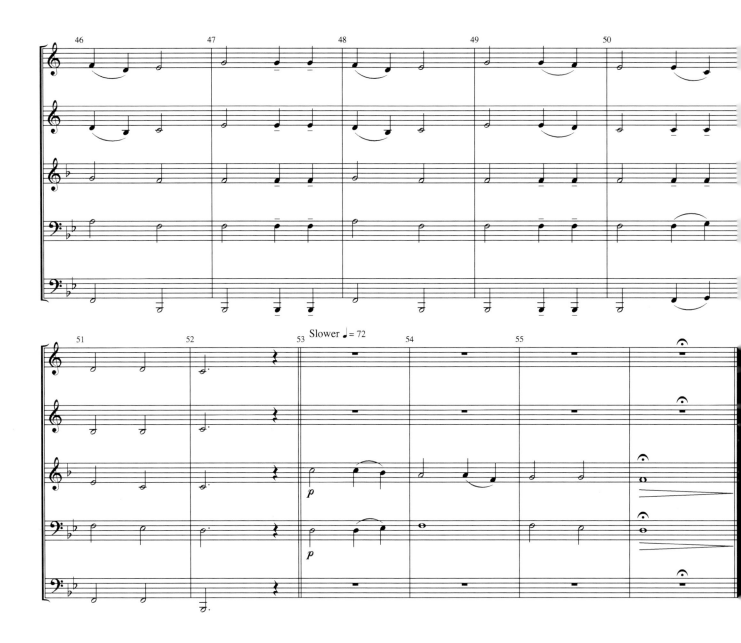